DSDM® - PROJE MANAGEMENT - A (STILL) UNKNOWN ALTERNATIVE FULL OF ADVANTAGES

AN INTRODUCTION TO THE AGILEPM® METHOD, WHICH COMBINES THE BEST OF CLASSICAL PROJECT MANAGEMENT AND AGILE PRODUCT DEVELOPMENT

ROBERT M. RICHARDS

Contents

Contents

Foreword

When I talk to customers and clients about agile approaches and methods, I always hear the prejudice after a very short time that they are all well and good, but that they are probably more suitable for companies that would implement any new ideas as a start-up on a greenfield site. In an environment like theirs, with all the divisions and departments and all the governance and controlling requirements, this would only be possible with considerable adjustments - if at all. Yes, there was a lot of good stuff in there and they had also used some agile ideas, but that was enough. We are not a start-up, but a stable company with solid values and clear processes. Rather, what is needed is a hybrid process management that encompasses the best of both worlds: flexibility and rapid value generation on the one hand, and planning, management, control and reporting on the other.

In fact, some agile frameworks do not emphasize the representation of process or organizational interfaces to the organization in their representations and this could be seen as a shortcoming. In most cases, however, this approach is simply due to the fact that a generic approach that is intended to cover different types as well as different complexities and sizes of product development simply cannot demand a single path and general interfaces and processes. Rather, it is up to the implementing organization to determine the appropriate customizations and process interfaces. This is actually normal when using any project approach and is part of the framework. The difference may simply be that some actually include a project management structure, while others focus on the core business, often "product development".

When I got to know AgilePM resp. DSDM a few years ago, I realized that it is a complete project method, which meets all requirements, even of large organizations, but is completely agile. You could say that it is the prototype of what some organizations understand under the keyword "hybrid project management", without being a "patchwork", as many hybrid approaches cobbled together from various frameworks are.

In this booklet I would like to give you a first insight into the DSDM method, which should allow the reader to find out for himself whether its approach is of interest for his own challenges. If you decide to use DSDM, I would like to recommend a suitable training as well as support by experts, who will support you in the introduction and the first projects with DSDM.

Personally, I believe that there are very few projects for which the DSDM approach is not suitable. However, I am happy to leave the decision up to you and am pleased if I have been able to arouse your interest in this outstanding project management method.

The author

Preliminary Note

DSDM® (stands for Dynamic System Development Method) and AgilePM® are both trademarks of Agile Business Consortium Limited (www.agilebusiness.org). This book has been produced independently of the copyright holder and represents the author's personal experience with the named method. In the text, the ® signs have been omitted for ease of reading. They should be kept in mind when reading.

ONE
INTRODUCTION TO AGILITY

Agility in our context is a general style of working. Projects are viewed holistically and are not just a set of deployment techniques.

It has always been one of the biggest challenges in any development to make sure that what you develop actually meets the needs of the customer.

Solving this problem was one of the motivations for the Agile Manifesto. The first guiding principle of the Agile Manifesto is: "Our highest priority is to satisfy the customer by delivering valuable results early and continuously."

In a fast-paced environment, Agile ensures solutions meet business needs and focuses on on-time delivery.

Delaying decisions as much as possible until they are based on facts rather than uncertain assumptions and predictions is fundamental to an agile approach. This does not mean that no planning should be required - on the contrary, planning activities should focus on the various options and adapt to the current situation as well as clarify confusing situations by creating an environment in which action can be taken quickly.

Agile is all about flexibility. The principle of responding to change according to a plan is seen as a strength of Agile. This does not mean that Agile makes planning obsolete. Things change, and you want to have flexibility to adapt and respond to those changes. You clearly want to have a plan for where you are going and approximately how you are going to get there. But you also want to leave room to adjust your plan.

The "Agile Manifesto

In February 2001, seventeen people met in a ski lodge in the Wasatch Mountains of the American state of Utah to talk, ski, and relax together. They were all dissatisfied with the way software development was taking place and believed that alternatives to documentation-heavy, heavyweight software development processes were needed.

This group of organizational anarchists, who called themselves "The Agile Alliance", jointly formulated and signed the "Agile Manifesto". It should be noted that the people present later went quite different ways and developed different methods and frameworks based on the common foundation "Agile Manifesto". (Co-)developers of "Extreme Programming", "Scrum", "DSDM", "Adaptive Software Development", "Crystal" and others laid here a common foundation for the further unfolding of software development and in many cases also for issues far beyond software development.

For more information on the history of its creation, please visit: http://agilemanifesto.org/history.html

Manifesto for Agile Software Development

We are uncovering better ways of developing
software by doing it and helping others do it.
Through this work we have come to value:

Individuals and interactions over processes and tools
Working software over comprehensive documentation
Customer collaboration over contract negotiation
Responding to change over following a plan

That is, while there is value in the items on
the right, we value the items on the left more.

Kent Beck
Mike Beedle
Arie van Bennekum
Alistair Cockburn
Ward Cunningham
Martin Fowler
James Grenning
Jim Highsmith
Andrew Hunt
Ron Jeffries

Jon Kern
Brian Marick
Robert C. Martin
Steve Mellor
Ken Schwaber
Jeff Sutherland
Dave Thomas

Individuals and interactions more than processes and tools

Following processes and using tools correctly is undoubtedly a key success factor for carrying out successful development processes. Nevertheless, the agile manifesto rightly places "individuals and interactions" in front of them. Only individuals are in a position to permanently evolve and thus achieve a constant improvement of the development process and the developed products. The interaction between individuals offers additional potential for the work of a team to become more than the sum of the individual performances. On the other hand, a team can only work optimally if each team member is also perceived as an individual with strengths, weaknesses and his or her own personality and is included as such.

Functioning software more than comprehensive documentation

Stipulating requirements in advance and documenting the implemented results are a basis for understanding product content and the foundation for successful maintenance and further development. However, if it is not possible to create a functioning software product, its usefulness is very limited.

Cooperation with the customer more than contract negotiation

Contracts and agreements between customers and manufacturers are of great importance. They form an important basis for ensuring that all parties understand an order in the same way. Nevertheless, contracts cannot depict every possible scenario in detail and anticipate every possible event. They are created based on the state of knowledge at a given point in time. In the course of a project, however, both the customer and the supplier continue to develop. The available knowledge about the joint project increases and the general conditions also change. In order to take this development into account in the project, good and intensive cooperation with the customer is an indispensable prerequisite.

Responding to change more than following a plan

Plans are important and the idea that agile approaches, such as Scrum, would do without plans is absurd. One could even say that there is far more planning in agile techniques. The main difference is that planning in an agile environment does not primarily take place at (or before) the start of the project, but on an ongoing basis and always with a "just in time" approach. It makes no sense to create detailed plans for months and years to come if you see customer feedback and responding to it as the basis for enabling maximum value-added development.

Twelve principles of the Agile Manifesto

First principle: "Our highest priority is to satisfy the customer by delivering valuable software early and continuously. »

Customer satisfaction is our highest priority. Through value-based prioritization in combination with the delivery of implemented solution parts already during the development process, we not only create the opportunity for more in-depth customer feedback at an early stage, but also contribute to the customer being able to realize benefits, if possible even before project completion.

Second principle: "Welcome requirement changes even late in development. Agile processes use change to the customer's

competitive advantage."

While in completely planned projects every change means a disruption, which possibly leads to weeks and months of intensive planning and coordination work having to be recreated, in agile development new and adapted requirements are not only planned for from the outset, but are also deliberately wanted. During the development of a product, both the client and the contractor continuously learn more about the product to be developed. The results of this learning process should not only be realized in a possible follow-up project or by means of later adaptation (after delivery), but should be incorporated into the development as early as possible. This can mean that already planned functionality has to be adapted or even omitted, or that completely new requirements suddenly have top priority. Only in this way are we able to provide our customer with the greatest possible benefit as soon as possible.

Third principle: "Deliver working software regularly within a few weeks or months, preferring the shorter time period."

Agile development is a joint effort between the contractor and the customer. While the contractor contributes its development resources, the client contributes its technical know-how and its knowledge of the existing or future desired processes. This joint development can be particularly successful if there is frequent and well-founded communication. This is fostered by frequent delivery and the resulting feedback. It gives the developer the opportunity to ensure that his product is evolving in the right direction, and provides the client with confidence that the product created will meet his requirements.

Fourth principle: "Subject matter experts and developers must work together on a daily basis during the project."

Agile software development is characterized by the ongoing exchange between subject matter experts and developers. This is not limited to the start of the project in the definition of requirements and at the end of the project in the acceptance of the solution, as is often the case with conventional project procedures. Collaboration takes place on an ongoing basis, whether in the definition of requirements and the corresponding acceptance criteria or then in feedback at the end of the iteration. In between, the involvement to clarify questions and requirements is also important.

Fifth principle: "Build projects around motivated individuals. Give them the environment and support they need and trust them to get the job done."

Agile software development cannot be successful if it is carried out by unmotivated people who work through lists of requirements. Rather, it is important that the developers see a purpose and benefit in their work and have the desire to produce something useful. This is the only way to ensure that optimal customer benefits are realized.

Sixth Principle: "The most efficient and effective way to communicate information to and within a development team is face-to-face."

Do you know the bad habit of communicating within teams via e-mails with the whole team as a distribution list? Everyone reads along somehow and everyone has the idea that they themselves are not actually meant. Communication science has long since proven that the pure wording is only a minimal part of the overall communication. Facial expressions/gestures, but also emphasis, contribute a much larger part to communication and understanding. Face-to-face communication offers many advantages: Use of all senses in communication (How did he/she mean that?), the possibility to ask back directly, information reaches the right addressee ...

Seventh principle: "Functioning software is the most important measure of progress."

A solution that is 99% implemented is still not ready and probably not usable in this way. Without in-depth analysis, it is hardly possible to say whether software is now 90 % or 70 % implemented - and even if it is: What benefit - one could also ask "what value" - does this solution have for the customer? Only completed, functioning software offers the intended benefit. What does not meet the requirements for the completed software (acceptance criteria, definition of "done") at the end of an iteration falls back into the work queue (product backlog) and can be implemented in a later iteration.

Eighth principle: "Agile processes promote sustainable development. Principals, developers, and users should be able to maintain a steady pace indefinitely."

Software development often takes place at the physical and mental limits of the developers, especially before deadlines. This can not only lead to health restrictions, but is often also the cause of errors and a lack of employee motivation. If the development team can work at a steady pace, this not only has a positive impact on long-term employee satisfaction and willingness to perform, but also on the quality of the products created.

Ninth principle: "Constant attention to technical excellence and good design promotes agility."

The abandonment of extended design before the start of implementation does not mean that no value would be placed on solid software design and high quality. Unlike conventional approaches, both only evolve with the requirements in the course of development. This must be taken into account from the very beginning. This is the only way to ensure that constraints in the selected software architecture do not arise during the course of the project that make it difficult or even impossible to implement customer feedback.

Tenth principle: "Simplicity - the art of maximizing the amount of work not done - is essential."

The goal of agile software development is not to develop the largest possible functional scope within a short time or at low cost. Rather, the central goal is to achieve the greatest possible value creation for the customer with the least possible development effort and the least possible developed software. This can only be achieved if there is a clear idea of which requirements result in which added value for the company. Based on this, requirements are prioritized and implemented (or not) accordingly.

Eleventh principle: "The best architectures, requirements, and designs come from self-organized teams."

When an experienced team of developers comes together, it can be assumed that together they have a higher level of experience and knowledge than an individual has. Accordingly, it makes sense to give this team the necessary freedom for their development project, i.e. as much freedom as possible with regard to the approach and the structure of the implementation, insofar as this supports or optimizes the benefit for the customer.

Twelfth principle: "Periodically, the team reflects on how it can become more effective and adjusts its behavior accordingly."

Continuous improvement is a central concern of agile software development. This applies not only to the product created, but also to the way the team works and cooperates. Accordingly, it is important that the team regularly examines the development process and cooperation within the team and jointly looks for ways to improve. This benefits both the team itself and the services provided by the team.

TWO

AGILEPM - BASICS

The elements of DSDM

DSDM is an agile project management approach that can be optimally adapted to corporate project environments of varying complexity and size. Its structure ensures that - when applied correctly - the project organization and the resources spent on it are always kept within a reasonable framework. To ensure this, there is a multi-stage phase model with clear tasks and goals as well as resources.

'Enough Design Up Front' (EDUF).

Within the framework of the DSDM phase model, a fundamental understanding is developed in the pre-project phase to clarify the structure of the intended solution. This provides the basis for an informed decision as to whether further pursuit of the project is goal-oriented and beneficial.

In the positive case, the project is started with the feasibility phase. Here, it is determined whether the project is feasible from a technical point of view and can also satisfy entrepreneurial criteria. Just enough effort is expended to decide whether further steps make sense.

In the subsequent phase, the Foundations phase, further foundations are developed. Here, a basic understanding of the benefits of the project (business case), development and solution approaches, project organizations, requirements and a rough delivery plan are created.

Such a procedure is indeed very reminiscent of the one that Prince2® also knows and the respective methodology must certainly also be seen in context with each other. One has influenced the other. However, we will still see that despite certain overlaps, there are also significant differences and DSDM is a truly independent approach, which is considerably superior to the current version of Prince2® (V. 2017) in terms of the implementation of agile principles in many respects and rightly positions itself as "Agile Project Management".

Once the foundations have been laid and development has begun, the project enters an iterative lifecycle in which products are developed in short, focused periods of time (timeboxes). Clearly defined results are achieved in each timebox, which are then delivered / put into operation in deployment phases.

DSDM is based on eight principles that promote a deeper understanding of the method and provide a guiding ray for DSDM project decisions.

The benefits of DSDM for project success

The idea that in a project of a certain complexity all customer requirements are already available in their final form at the start of the project is wrong in the vast majority of cases. We live in a rapidly changing world in which framework conditions such as laws, the market situation, customer requirements, technical conditions and many other things are constantly changing. In addition, it has been shown time and again that misunderstandings and different assessments of situations actually occur in all projects. If we now assume that framework conditions change in various respects over time, it is to be expected that from a certain - not too high - degree of complexity, the possibility of predicting these changes (and their interactions) is limited. Accordingly, in traditional waterfall projects, where all (or most) of the planning work is done at the beginning of the project, it must almost inevitably be expected that adjustments to deliverables will occur either during the project or in subsequent change requests. Accordingly, it is important to use a method that assumes the possibility of changes as a given right at the beginning and responds to them in a targeted manner as part of the methodology. Such an approach is called "Agile".

In the context of many projects, however, the idea of what many people understand as "agile" does not seem desirable. A certain degree of planning security is necessary, and it must be possible to clearly agree on framework conditions. Funders and the organization are not willing to hope for a maximized business value that is not further determined. Contracts and agreements want to be concluded and, if necessary, even tenders should be issued. This requires a certain degree of clear framework conditions. This is exactly where DSDM offers extremely successful solutions. DSDM stands for "agile product development on a solid foundation", supported by a clearly structured process and role model and a goal-oriented project management approach.

An important success factor of an agile project is a project management that sees itself less as a classic manager who leads his team to best performance via "command and control", but rather as a moderator who strengthens his team and allows it to grow in order to enable the team to decide for itself within an appropriate scope and only escalates decisions in the case of exceptions.

Projects and project variables

Introduction

DSDM's philosophy is, "The greatest business value occurs when projects are aligned with clear business objectives, deliver regular results, and involve the collaboration of motivated and empowered people." [1]

For this philosophy to be successful, some basic requirements are necessary. First, it is necessary that the business objectives are communicated and understood. This is the only way to enable employees to make decisions for themselves. The regular delivery of results is used, on the one hand, to achieve initial business benefits before the project is completed, if possible, and, on the other hand, to learn from the experience gained with the partial deliveries and to make adjustments to the project accordingly. All of this, however, is carried out by people who are motivated and see meaning in their participation in the project. This way of managing projects therefore requires a certain lived image of people and a certain way of working together within an organization. The eight principles of DSDM set a framework for the successful implementation of projects. They are supported by people (with defined roles and responsibilities), an agile process, clearly defined document products and recommended practices.

Understanding project variables

Projects operate in a field of tension between different requirements. The most important are: Time, Cost, Features and Quality. Trying to fix all four at the beginning of a project is unrealistic, but many projects still try. This can work in a perfect world where requirements never change. Many projects fail when trying to master this balancing act.

In classic projects, the functional content (scope) is defined within the framework of specifications or requirements catalogs. Times and costs are determined on this basis. They can change in the course of the project due to external influences, errors and the like. If deviations are detected, additional resources are often deployed, which has an impact on costs and completion dates. In some cases, attempts are made to compensate for such delays by accelerating tests, which in turn can have an impact on the quality of the deliverables.

DSDM takes a different approach here. In a DSDM project, we set time, cost and quality and see functionality (scope) as a variable. So if the project goes over time or over budget, the lower priority requirements are dropped or deferred. Also note that the quality is also fixed, so you can be sure that the features provided will work as expected. An important reason for this approach lies in the experience that situations can arise from late delivery or going over budget that negatively impact the meaningfulness and usefulness of a project.

With the DSDM approach, we ensure that we can always deliver a viable solution on time and on budget (within budget) as long as feature prioritization and the time window are met. Delivery of a Minimum Viable Product (MVP) subset of requirements is guaranteed as a worst-case scenario.

By using acceptance criteria per deliverable, we ensure that the development team knows exactly what needs to be implemented, but can also focus on the requirements that are actually needed and does not implement unnecessary additional functionality. This takes into account the idea of solutions that are "just well enough" and counteracts the waste of project budget. If a deliverable meets all the requirements specified in the acceptance criteria, the development team can move on to the next requirement. If the situation arises during the project or a timebox (a development cycle) that not all planned requirements are implemented, it is already agreed in advance that, if necessary, requirements with lower priority can be deleted so that the timebox can be met as agreed.

For the DSDM approach to be carried out successfully, intensive collaboration between implementer and customer (whether internal or external) is necessary. This is the only way to ensure that specialist knowledge and technical expertise go hand in hand to realize maximum business benefits.

[1] _ AgilePM® Agile project management Handbook v2 - German Edition, UK, 2018

THREE

THE PRINCIPLES OF DSDM

Introduction

The DSDM philosophy is supported by eight principles. These form a basis for decisions and cooperation in DSDM projects. Even if the meaning and purpose of such principles may not be obvious at first glance, they play a central role and their compliance represents the actual success factor of DSDM. Like any project management methodology, DSDM is not able to define and describe all situations that may occur in a project, and even if this were possible, such an approach would not be purposeful. Rather, the success of DSDM is based on the fact that those involved in the project can make decisions within the scope of their competencies and activities, and for this it is necessary to have common goals, but also a common set of values and rules. These are supported by the DSDM philosophy and the eight principles. The 8 principles are:

1. Focus on the business need
2. Deliver on time
3. Work together
4. Do not tolerate any compromise in terms of quality
5. Build step by step on solid foundations
6. Develop iteratively
7. Communicate continuously and clearly
8. Demonstrate control

Principle 1 - Focus on the business need

Meeting the business need of a project must always be considered during the project. Decisions are to be made in such a way that they optimally support this need.

Prerequisites are:

- The project team understands business professionals.
- A valid, understandable business case exists, which is known to the stakeholders within the scope of their activities and decision span.
- The project is supported by the company and positioned accordingly.
- There is general agreement with the view that not all requirements will be implemented, but only those with the highest priorities, as far as this is feasible within the defined dimensions (cost / time / quality).
- There is a continuous exchange of all persons involved in the project.

Principle 2 - Deliver on time

In many cases, it is not only a success factor that a certain product is manufactured, but also that it is available at a certain point in time. For example, it can be crucial for market success that a certain product is available before a competitor's product, or a certain product must be able to be used at a certain point in time because it will subsequently no longer be of use or no longer be of use to the same extent. Accordingly, it is important to meet deadlines under all circumstances.

Prerequisites are:

- Division of work into manageable work packages
- Prioritization based on business benefit
- Acquiring confidence in delivery readiness through positive prior experience in previous work packages / timeboxes.
- Reliable estimation and continuous learning from past estimation experiences.
- Clear communication

Principle 3 - Work together

An important factor in the success of multiple people working together to achieve a common goal is whether the people truly see themselves as a team or just a community of fate working to achieve the same goal. Working together as a team fosters better understanding, greater speed, and shared ownership that allows teams to work at a level that exceeds the sum of their parts and is much more productive.

Prerequisite for this is:

- Build a team culture and take care to strengthen it in the long term
- Promote appreciative, open communication
- Involve stakeholders and company representatives at the right time and encourage their proactive participation
- Promote team motivation and identification with project goals
- Ensure that all members of the team are empowered to make decisions on behalf of the people they represent. There is no room for micromanagement in AgilePM.

Principle 4 - Don't compromise on quality

In DSDM projects, the quality level to be achieved is agreed at the start of the project. All work aims to implement the deliverables at this level. The aim is not to achieve maximum quality, but a quality level that is just "good enough", i.e. that meets the agreed requirements. Anything beyond that would incur unnecessary costs. The perfect solution is often too expensive.

Prerequisite for this is:

- Clear agreements, understood by all parties, exist on the level of quality to be achieved before development begins
- Early and continuous testing at the agreed level
- Quality assurance is lived as part of the development process
- Ensure that all requirements have quality objectives in the form of acceptance criteria that are understandable and consistent with the overall goal.

Principle 5 - Build progressively on solid foundations

Unlike some other agile approaches, DSDM emphasizes approaching projects based on a solid foundation. This is done by first creating a clear, shared understanding of the function, intended benefits, scope of work, and estimated costs. This not only provides a solid basis for decision-making that enables consensus to be reached on what the project needs to deliver, but also provides a planning basis against which the project can be compared as it progresses.

By developing step-by-step and delivering (partial) business results as early as possible, not only early value creation is enabled. Step-by-step delivery can also strengthen the trust of stakeholders and their feedback can create the opportunity for adjustments during the project.

Prerequisite for this are:

- Analysis and design in a depth and detail appropriate to the project phase
- Formal reassessment of priorities and informal reassessment of ongoing project feasibility with each increment delivered.

Principle 6 - Develop iteratively

Iterative development means that the same development process, often a sequence of design, programming, testing and documentation, runs completely in each individual development cycle, called timeboxes in DSDM. Iteration means "repetition." Since this means that the entire development process for deliverables runs (which also includes quality assurance), there is a higher probability of achieving quality targets and, based on demonstrations of the solutions, also of recognizing changed requirements at an early stage and incorporating these into the further development process. This means that the implementation of requirements can move closer and closer to a desired goal and, where necessary, can be adjusted or counteracted at short notice.

Prerequisite for this is:

- A mindset that welcomes and incorporates feedback and new requirements during the project

- Transparency
- A planning aimed at a gradual development
- Regular interaction between development and stakeholder/client
- Understanding of the development process as one that involves creativity, experimentation, learning and adaptation (CIP - Continuous Improvement Process).

Principle 7 - Communicate continuously and clearly

A central success factor for any type of project is good communication between those directly involved in the project and between project staff and stakeholders. DSDM is designed to support this communication. However, it is also critical to success. Accordingly, it is important to demand communication and cooperation from the stakeholders when this is not taking place as required.

Prerequisite for this is:

- Informal face-to-face communication at all levels
- Conduct and actively participate in daily team stand-up meeting with stakeholders.
- Use of moderated and well-prepared meetings and workshops
- Use of aids to promote communication
- Transparency and openness
- Early presentation of solutions and open communication about them
- Lean, up-to-date communication
- Feedback from the right stakeholders (those who are competent for the specific issue)
- Respectful interaction with each other

Principle 8 - Demonstrate control

Complex projects required continuous control at all levels. This should correspond to the current project phase in every case. In order not to slide into the need for micromanagement as a result, transparency is crucial. Reporting, control and documentation must be appropriate and correspond to the goal to be achieved.

Prerequisite for this is:

- Phase-dependent design of plans
- Transparent planning and progress review
- Product-oriented progress measurement (not activity-based)
- Regular monitoring of the congruence of project progress and business objectives
- Use an appropriate level of formality for tracking and reporting
- Refrain from blaming and focus on constructive aspects

FOUR

ISF'S - INSTRUMENTAL SUCCESS FACTORS

The ISFS, in German WEFs, the essential success factors of DSDM, are central elements of the DSDM methodology. If they cannot be met, this represents a significant project risk and requires appropriate measures to be taken immediately:

- Acceptance of the DSDM approach
- An effective solution development team
- Entrepreneurial commitment - active and continuous
- Iterative development, integrated testing and step-by-step implementation
- Transparency

Acceptance of the DSDM approach

In order to successfully implement a methodology, it is essential that the stakeholders accept the method and are willing to engage in the associated processes, roles and responsibilities. If we now start from the DSDM approach, it is very important that all stakeholders agree that the approach is not based on completely working through a list of requirements, but on safely creating from the existing requirements those that offer maximum added value for the client, and furthermore, based on prioritization, those that are possible within the available time and financial budget. This circumstance should be clearly coordinated in particular with the client /

sponsor of the project.

An effective solution development team

People are at the heart of successful AgilePM projects, and the solution development team is key to ensuring the right solution is developed. Important success factors here are:

- Decision-making authority
- Stability (changes in the team always lead to performance losses)
- Presence of the required knowledge and skills
- Team size that enables self-organized collaboration. DSDM speaks here of 7 +/- 2 people (i.e. 5-9 people).

Each role on the solution development team should be empowered to make decisions based on their expertise, and the entire team should be empowered to make decisions within the boundaries agreed upon during inception. There is no room for micromanagement in DSDM. This freedom to make decisions should not be seen as a free pass, but rather as a mandate to recognize and exercise responsibility within the limits of one's own responsibility and task. The corresponding limits of freedom of decision must be reconciled within the framework of the project.

Entrepreneurial commitment - active and continuous

The existence of suitable framework conditions is essential for the successful implementation of a project. This includes, in particular, comprehensive and sustainable support from the company. Particular mention should be made here of the following:

- The consistent commitment and observance of working hours
- Active involvement of business functions in solution development, especially through technical input
- A supportive commercial relationship

Iterative development, integrated testing and step-by-step implementation

Many classic projects suffer from considerable quality restrictions. This is often due to the fact that tests are carried out very late in the course of the project and are used by some organizations as a kind of buffer in order to meet deadlines that are actually no longer sustainable. In combination with an often also late presentation of often already very extensive (interim) events to the client, this results in a high project risk.

Agile project management methods and especially DSDM address this problem by dividing the implementation into small, clear solution cycles (in DSDM these are called timeboxes, in Scrum they are called sprints). Each of these solution cycles is always complete, i.e., all required implementation steps from analysis to implementation, testing, integration and documentation are just as much a part of the cycle as the presentation of the solution and the receipt of feedback from the stakeholders.

Thus, for all types of projects, early testing reduces the risk of detecting deeply embedded errors, which can take a lot of time and effort to fix, too late to take appropriate corrective action.

An important advantage of this approach, and in particular of the fact that testing is part of the development cycles, is that partial solutions are available for delivery more quickly and can thus already generate initial benefits during the project runtime. Not to be underestimated is the fact that solutions that are used productively also lead to faster feedback from users, which in turn can lead to faster responses to them, thus significantly reducing project risk and increasing user confidence in the solution.

The concept of incremental delivery also extends to individual timeboxes, with each timebox ideally delivering a complete potentially implementable increment of the solution. When the Business Ambassador accepts requirements as "done" at the end of a timebox, this provides assurance that a Solution Increment truly meets business expectations, even though sufficient functionality may not have been implemented at that point to physically put it into operation.

Transparency

Agile methods such as DSDM are based on the collaboration of the people and organizations involved. This can only be successful if there is a high degree of transparency that allows everyone to think along and contribute their viewpoints and knowledge. To this end, both the current work and the implemented solutions are presented openly and transparently. This is explicitly not about "project marketing", where positive aspects are often strongly emphasized and difficulties are omitted as much as possible. Trust is based on openness, and only when problems and difficulties are also openly addressed and presented is there a basis for trusting and sustainable cooperation.

AgilePM is about building trust in the evolving solution and in this way reducing the risks of the unknown or unseen. The value of building trust through incremental delivery of business value, ideally demonstrating fully completed requirements / user stories (created, tested and accepted by the business) at the end of each timebox, cannot be underestimated. If this cannot be achieved, an alternative demonstration of progress may be required.

FIVE
THE DSDM PROCESS

DSDM successfully combines the advantages of iterative product development, as is also known in other agile approaches, with those of classic project management. Thus, a relatively linear structure of pre-project - development of project bases and plans - delivery and operation embeds an iterative development part, which, however, also leads to the fact that the delivery process can be run through several times. Thus, the requirements of an organization for project management in terms of control and administration can be ideally combined with the advantages of a development process focused on learning and value maximization. Thus, one could say that DSDM - although it is a fully-fledged agile method - has succeeded in fulfilling all the common requirements that have many companies calling for "hybrid project management".

Although DSDM itself is designed as a complete project management methodology, which is able to cover all processes of the development project, it is one of the strengths of the method not to close itself to the combination with other methods such as Prince2, PMI or software development methods such as eXtreme Programming (XP) or Kanban.

Pre-Project Phase

The pre-project phase ensures that only the right projects are started and set up correctly based on a clearly defined objective.

Feasibility phase

In the feasibility phase, the project idea is to be examined from a technical and business perspective. On the one hand, to determine whether the proposed project is likely to be feasible from a technical point of view, and then whether it has a positive cost-benefit ratio from a business point of view. The effort associated with feasibility should be just sufficient to determine whether further investigation is warranted or whether the project should be stopped now because it is probably not feasible or not economically feasible. Stopping a project that does not make sense at this time should not be seen as a "failure" but as a measure of responsibility.

Foundation Phase

The Foundations phase continues the project feasibility research begun in the Feasibility phase. The goal is to build a better understanding of the reasons for the project, the potential solution that will be created by the project, and the development management and delivery of the solution. The Foundations phase should have an appropriate scope and useful level of detail. The scope should not exceed one week, even for large and complex projects. The further details will only take place in the subsequent evolutionary development and that only for the next phase in each case.

In rare cases, it may be necessary to schedule a new Foundations phase after a Deployment phase if it becomes apparent that key fundamentals will change during the course of the project or if a Deployment has led to an unforeseen result and it is therefore advisable to adjust the planning fundamentals.

In small, simple projects, Feasibility Phase and Foundations Phase can coincide.

The Foundations phase also includes determining how DSDM will be adapted to the project environment.

Evolutionary Development Phase

In the evolutionary development phase, the solution is developed within the framework of iterative development phases. The methods and tools used here are timeboxes, MoSCoW prioritization, and workshops, with the help of which the picture of the created solution becomes more and more complete.

Deployment phase

In the deployment phase, a (partial) solution of the evolving solution that has been realized up to this point is put into operation. This has multiple benefits. On the one hand, an initial realization of benefits should take place as early as possible, and on the other hand, the commissioning phase also offers the opportunity to draw knowledge from the experience gained in real use, which can be fed back into development and enable an even better, more mature product to be produced.

The deployment phase comprises three main activities: Integration of the already implemented solution parts, review and the actual delivery.

Post-Project Phase

After the last deployment of a project has taken place and thus the developed solution has been delivered, the project is completed and the post-project phase follows.

Now it is a matter of realizing the business benefits forecast for the project and comparing the benefits actually achieved with those planned.

In the post-project phase, one or more benefit assessments are created for these realized benefits in relation to the business case. The benefit can be created for individual releases (in which case the benefit assessment should begin before the post-project phase is reached), for the entire project, or omitted entirely, depending on the requirements of the organization.

SIX

ROLES AND RESPONSIBILITIES

Positive, goal-oriented cooperation between people with different skills and tasks is a central factor in the success of projects. This is made possible by having a clear distribution of roles and the associated responsibilities. DSDM divides roles into four categories:

- Roles with business interests
- Roles with solution-specific / technical interests
- Roles with management interests
- Roles with process interests

The best solutions result from self-organizing empowered teams. However, these teams and the people in them must actively take responsibility for their empowerment within agreed-upon boundaries. Prerequisites for this are:

- Mutual respect
- Assuming responsibility
- Courage to tackle new approaches to improve solutions and collaboration in a sustainable way.

In addition to the orientation (focus) of the roles, DSDM also distinguishes the roles according to the nature of their contribution to the project:

- Roles at project level
- Roles of the Solution Development Team
- Supporting roles

Roles at project level

Project level roles are together for project control. They cooperate with the management outside the project.

The Business Sponsor provides the overall strategic direction and controls the funding/budget for the project. The Business Visionary and Technical Coordinator hold the business and technical visions for the project, respectively. The Project Manager ensures that project funds are used effectively to deliver the planned solution within the agreed upon timeframe. The Business Analyst is the link to the Solution Development Team level and part of both levels.

The project level roles are:

- Business Sponsor
- Business Visionary
- Technical Coordinator
- Project Manager
- Business Analyst

Roles of the Solution Development Team

It is these roles that provide the concrete development within the project. They design and build the solution and are jointly responsible for its daily development and for ensuring its suitability for business purposes.

There may be one or more Solution Development Teams within a project. Each team includes all roles of the Solution Development Team and covers all responsibilities.

The membership of each solution development team should be stable during a project. However, in the worst case scenario, each solution development team should remain stable for one project increment. Each member of the solution development team is an empowered individual who takes responsibility for their area of responsibility and represents the interests of their colleagues.

The roles of the Solution Development Team are:

- Business Ambassador
- Solution Developer
- Solution Tester
- Business Analyst (at the same time also on project level)
- Team Leader

Supporting roles

Supporting roles provide support and guidance to the project on an ad hoc basis throughout the lifecycle. They collaborate with the project as needed. For example, a business or technical consultant is involved during the Foundations phase when their expertise is required to properly shape the evolving solution. Consultants can be staffed by multiple people, for example, with different subject matter expertise.

The supporting roles are:

- Business Advisors
- Technical Advisors
- Workshop Facilitator
- DSDM Coach

SEVEN

THE INDIVIDUAL ROLES AND THEIR RESPONSIBILITIES

Roles with business focus

Business Sponsor

The role of the Business Sponsor is the most senior role in the project. He is or represents the client and is therefore the final decision maker. He is specifically responsible for the business case and the project budget and also has a sufficiently high position outside the project organization to be able to solve business problems and make financial decisions.

This role has a critical responsibility to ensure and enable rapid progress throughout the project. To do this, he must be available throughout the project, but does not need to interfere in the day-to-day business (which often would not be possible based on his high position in the organization already in terms of time).

For larger projects or in complex organizations, the financial responsibility of the business sponsor may be held by a higher authority such as an investment board or executive committee, most of which will then appoint a representative from its ranks to be the business sponsor. This ensures that the project deals with a single final decision maker and a single final escalation point.

Business Visionary

The Business Visionary is responsible within the business organization for maintaining and pursuing a single, clear vision. The role is only ever performed by a single person.

The Business Visionary is more actively involved than the Business Sponsor and is responsible for interpreting the Business Sponsor's needs, communicating them to the team, and ensuring they are properly represented in the business case, as appropriate.

The Business Visionary remains accountable throughout the project. It is he or she who provides strategic direction to the team and ensures that the evolving solution meets the business case and can deliver the agreed benefits. At the end of the project, the Business Visionary owns the solution provided and is responsible for realizing the associated benefits.

Business Advisor

The Business Advisor is asked to provide specific and often specialized input into solution development or testing. The Business Advisor is typically an intended user or beneficiary of the solution or may be a representative of a focus group. The Business Advisor may also provide legal or regulatory advice as needed.

Business Ambassador

The Business Ambassador is the primary representative of the business requirements within the Solution Development Team. Accordingly, he must have the authority and knowledge to fulfill this responsibility.

During the Foundations phase, the Business Ambassador makes an important contribution to creating and prioritizing the requirements. He then supports the development team with details on the individual requirements. Where his own experience does not allow this, he can also draw on the knowledge of the Business Advisor. In day-to-day business, the Business Ambassador is the ambassador for the business organization and as such has decision-making authority. In order for this to happen, care must be taken when selecting the Business Ambassador to choose a person who is both competent and has decision-making authority. At the same time, the person must also have the maturity to decide where his or her own knowledge and competence are sufficient and where support from the business advisor is needed.

In most projects, the Business Ambassador's commitment is part-time at a level agreed upon during the Foundations phase. In order to ensure that the Business Ambassador can devote the required attention to the project, it is necessary in most cases to relieve him of his daily business outside the project.

Business Analyst

The Business Analyst connects the roles at the project level with those at the Solution Development Team level. He also balances the business and technical view of the project and ensures appropriate decisions about the evolving solution. He ensures the balance not as a mediator, but by facilitating communication between the stakeholders. He ensures that the business requirements are properly modeled and analyzed and correctly reflected in the guidance the team needs to build the solution. The active involvement of business users in the process of evolving the solution is critical to the success of a DSDM project.

Roles with management focus

Project Manager

The role of the Project Manager is a management role. His/her role is not day-to-day, but to ensure the framework in which the Solution Development Team can develop the solution. The Project Manager also coordinates all aspects of project management at a coarse level. In keeping with the DSDM concept of empowerment, the project manager is expected to leave the detailed planning of product development to the members of the Solution Development Team. Accordingly, the management style should be less command and control and more empowerment. This enables the team to make decisions and bear responsibility.

The role does not require any particular professional or technical ability, although neither is a hindrance. However, this may vary in different projects and project environments. The project manager can come from the business or solution-oriented / technical side. In projects where the customer-supplier relationship goes beyond companies, a project may have a project manager from both the customer and supplier side.

It is common for the project manager to take responsibility for the entire duration of the project. This must include both business and technical aspects of the project.

Team Leader

The Team Leader ideally acts as a servant-leader for the Solution Development Team, ensuring that it functions as a whole and achieves its goals. The Team Leader works with the team to plan and coordinate all aspects of product delivery at a detailed level. The role should be thought of as more of a "team captain" than a manager. Accordingly, it has proven effective if the role holder is chosen by the team itself for this purpose. In some projects, it has also proven successful to swap this role among the members of the Solution Development Team during the course of projects, for example based on the specific requirements of a timebox.

The roles with technical focus

Technical Coordinator

As the technical authority of the project, the Technical Coordinator ensures that the solution / technical roles function consistently, that the project is technically coherent, and that it meets the desired technical standards. The Technical Coordinator has the same role in technical terms as the Business Visioray in business terms.

Technical Advisor

The Technical Advisor is the technical equivalent of the Business Advisor with regard to technical issues. He supports, for example, with questions regarding technical feasibility, change management and maintenance aspects.

Business Analyst

In DSDM, the role of the business analyst is assigned to both the business focus and the technical focus. It has already been described in the context "Business Focus".

Solution Developer

The Solution Developers work with the other roles in the Solution Development Team to interpret the requirements and implement them in these corresponding products. This requires both technical knowledge and the willingness and ability to make decisions at the day-to-day level. Solution developers should be assigned to the project on a full-time basis. If this is not the case, it can lead to significant problems in meeting timeboxes, which represents a considerable project risk.

Solution Tester

The Solution Tester role is a role of the Solution Development Team. It performs tests that arise throughout the project and, in particular, also works with the business roles to ensure that the tests also meet the business requirements. It informs the Team Leader about the test results.

Roles with process focus

Workshop Facilitator

The workshop facilitator is responsible for all processes related to the organization and delivery of workshops. The facilitator is responsible for organizing and conducting a session that enables participants to achieve the workshop objective. The workshop facilitator should be independent of the outcomes to be achieved in the workshop.

DSDM Coach

The person who takes on the task of DSDM coach must have experience with DSDM. It is he or she who supports the team in using DSDM in the best possible way and thus being able to work together effectively. If necessary, the DSDM can also intervene to change framework conditions that hold the team back and remove obstacles.

EIGHT

METHODS AND TECHNIQUES

Of course, a wide variety of methods and techniques are applicable in the context of DSDM, and their use may vary depending on the project topic, scope, and intended benefits.

In addition, there are some methods and techniques prescribed by DSDM as part of the methodology, the use of which can be seen as a prerequisite for a project to be called a DSDM project.

MoSCoW - Prioritization

MoSCoW is a key technique for understanding priorities. Prioritization can be applied to requirements, tasks, products, user stories, acceptance criteria, and testing. This is about prioritization in relation to requirements.

The letters stand for:

- **M** (must haves) must have - represents requirements whose delivery must be guaranteed, because without them the project would not have the intended benefits and accordingly would not be justified.
- **S** (should have) represents requirements that are to be delivered to the best of our ability. If the case arises that a requirement is not implemented, this does not call the project benefit into question, but it does lead to additional work, e.g. workarounds.

- **C** (Could have) could have - requirements that are highly desirable, but whose implementation is less important than with the should have's.
- **W** (Won't have this time) not this time - requirements which are currently not implemented.

The MoSCoW technique is designed to guarantee delivery of the minimum usable subset. As a rule of thumb, the Must Haves should not account for more than 60% of the effort. The Should Haves and Could Haves each account for 20%. This corresponds to a contingency of 40%, which allows for even the most optimistic estimates.

Throughout the project, priorities must be continually reviewed as understanding of depth and detail changes.

Although the minimum usable subset is guaranteed, most projects are expected to meet the requirements. The delivery of the coulds is always considered a bonus and a delivery that only implements the musts is considered a worst case scenario.

Timeboxing

Timeboxing is one of the key techniques in agile project management. A timebox is a well-defined process for controlling the iterative creation of products at the detailed level. Verification points ensure that products are produced with the right quality.

The recommended period for a timebox is 2-6 weeks. This is not mandatory, but it is recommended to keep it as short as possible. 2-3 weeks is more typical.

At the beginning of each Timebox there is always a Kick Off. This is a short session, usually 1-3 hours, so that the Solution Development Team understands and accepts the Timebox goals as realistic.

A timebox contains three main stages: Investigation, Refinement and Consolidation.

During the investigation phase (Investigation), the details of the products and their measurement are agreed upon. This should take up to 10-20% of the timebox.

In the refinement phase, the main developments and tests are performed according to the agreed priorities. This should take 60-80% of the timebox.

Consolidation ties up the loose ends and ensures that all products meet their acceptance criteria. This should not take more than 10-20% of the timebox.

The timebox concludes with a close-out where the Business Visionary and Technical Coordinator formally accept the deliverables.

Each timebox schedule is created during the kick off.

An important method of communication and control is the Daily Stand-Up.

Iterative development

The definition of iterative development is: "A process in which the evolving solution, or part of it, moves from a concept to something with recognized business value." This is the key agile project management technique for evolving solutions from a high-level idea to a delivered solution. It is a process where repeated cycles of product development lead to an outcome that is closer to a desired outcome after each iteration.

The cycle usually requires that the team successively:

- Identifies what they need to accomplish in this iteration by having a conversation.
- Consider what is required and how to implement it.
- Executes the plan by creating the required product(s).
- Further discussions will then be held to review the outcome and determine if further work is required.

Iterations often start with prototypes or other tools (modeling), as a basis for joint solution development. Agility always means explorative approaches, where things are explored in the form of experiments and trials. If these are successful, new, better solutions emerge; if they are not, alternatives are sought or the tried and true is continued.

Iterative development encourages the Solution Development Team to work very cooperatively. Quality must be ensured at all times through early testing and immediate corrections when errors are discovered.

Modeling & Prototyping

"A picture is worth a thousand words." You could also say, "Models are a better way to communicate than large documents."

Agile methods, including DSDM, place great emphasis on approaches that make it possible to test new approaches with little effort and to facilitate communication between project participants through visualizations. Dozens of approaches and methods exist for this purpose, which are integrated to a greater or lesser extent in different frameworks.

The Solution Development Team should use modeling techniques to ensure effective communication between the business and technical staff.

A single model does not always cover all aspects of the project, as this could become too complicated. It usually focuses on the who, what, when, where, why or how.

Of course, the use and type of models vary from project to project, from a scale model of a new school to a quick hand-drawn sketch.

Facilitated Workshops

Facilitated workshops are a special type of meeting with a clear objective.

They have a workshop owner who needs and is the driver of the outcome, and they have participants who are empowered to make decisions. These workshops are facilitated by an independent facilitator who empowers and encourages participants to achieve an agreed goal.

Workshops are an important agile technique for fostering collaboration and effective communication. They can be used throughout the lifecycle and for a variety of reasons.

For example, for requirements gathering and prioritization, project kick-off, planning, defining the statement of work for each role, risk, and timebox reviews.

They do not replace meetings, but they offer a good and often better alternative, especially where the topic requires consensus and agreement.

The agile project manager may need to support the team by getting the right people to participate and ensuring that the budget allows for appropriate venues for workshops.

A project offers many advantages to using facilitated workshops. These include quick and quality decision making, better buy-in from all stakeholders, building team spirit, building consensus, and clarifying issues.

For the workshop to be effective, there are several success factors. These include: having a trained and independent workshop facilitator; not forcing decisions and agreements; and ensuring that participants receive a workshop report listing decisions and actions ideally within 48 hours of the workshop.

NINE

THE DSDM PRODUCTS IN THE COURSE OF THE PROJECT

At each stage of a project, products are produced, referenced or updated.

Product descriptions are generic in DSDM and should be adapted to the requirements of each organization and project. Be careful not to specify them too precisely so that the flexibility built into Agile is not lost. Not all products are needed for every project.

Some products are evolutionary, e.g. the Delivery Plan, where feasibility is created in outline and further details in basics. Others are milestone products - they are created specifically at a particular point in the lifecycle. For example, the Foundations Summary, which provides a snapshot of the business, the solution, and the company, or

Management products at the end of the Foundations phase.

Terms of Reference

The pre-project phase is about clarifying what needs to be investigated during feasibility. This phase is particularly important in larger organizations where such investigations need to be prioritized as part of a portfolio or program management.

Users of PRINCE2 will recognize a clear alignment with the "Starting Up a Project" process.

The business problem or opportunity must be identified. The project must be aligned with the business strategy. The work and resources required to complete the feasibility phase must be planned.

This phase should be kept as short as possible.

The main objective of the Terms of Reference is to capture and justify the feasibility investigation. It is likely to be a short document of no more than two pages, although in many organizations a simple email or even a verbal agreement is sufficient to allow a potential project to enter the feasibility phase.

Feasibility Assessment

During the Feasibility phase, the project manager works with the other project roles and especially the business analyst to determine if the project is feasible. The evolutionary products created here help define the work to be done and determine which of the six basic products (Business Case, Prioritized Requirements List, Solution Architecture Definition, Development Approach Definition, Delivery Approach, Management Approach Definition) need to be created as a concept. The Feasibility Assessment summarizes these findings and is a milestone that is presented to the business sponsor to assess whether the solution is likely to meet the business requirements. Not all business proposals make it to the Foundations phase.

The feasibility assessment presents the results of the feasibility phase to the business sponsor so that the company can decide whether there is sufficient justification for moving to the start-up phase. It summarizes all other products (described below) and can often take the form of a presentation.

Business Case

The business case provides a vision and business rationale for the project.

It describes the business as expected at the end of the project or at the end of each increment of the project. The business case is usually based on an investment appraisal that determines whether the value of the solution justifies the cost of producing it, supporting it, and balancing it against an acceptable level of risk. The business case is made in outline during the Feasibility phase and used to justify whether it is worth moving to the Foundations phase.

By the end of the Foundations phase, the project manager must ensure that the business case includes the vision, estimated costs, and any other analysis needed to justify the project. The business case should be strong enough to secure the investment and obtain adequate support from the business for the resources required to deliver the solution.

Prioritised Requirements List

During the Feasibility phase, the prioritized requirements list records the key requirements to be met by the project. The early indication of their MoSCoW priority is given in relation to the achievement of the objectives of the project, which are determined by the business requirements. A requirement describes a demand or a function that the user needs. No further details are planned at this stage. They will be further worked on and refined during later phases.

By the end of the Foundations phase, the project manager must ensure that the prioritized requirements list includes all the general requirements to be met by the project for at least the first increment. They must be detailed enough to fit more than one into a timebox. For each requirement, the acceptance criteria should be defined and MoSCoW priorities assigned. They must be sufficiently estimated so that total costs and deadlines can be determined at the end of the Foundations Phase. The Business Visionary must ensure that they represent adequate breadth to achieve the business benefits and then approve them.

Solution Architecture Definition

The Solution Architecture Definition describes the overall design framework for the solution from both a business and technical perspective and should begin to make the scope of the project clear. This can be a diagram at this early stage.

By the end of the Foundations phase, the project manager must then ensure that the Solution Architecture definition is sufficiently understood by the entire project management team, but especially by the Solution

Development team. It should help define the solution, but not so much that it limits the evolutionary nature of iterative development.

Development Approach Definition

The Development Approach Definition describes how the development team will work and what standards they will use, especially in terms of quality assurance and testing strategy. During the Feasibility phase, this can only refer to some already existing standards and how the Agile PM approach will be adapted.

During the Foundations phase, the project manager must ensure that the Solution Development Team understands and is fully committed to the way of working defined in the Development Approach Definition. This is often already documented in the organization's quality management system or in an existing quality plan. In this case, the project manager only needs to ensure that the team understands this.

Management Approach Definition

The Management Approach Definition is built during the Feasibility phase and addresses the approach to delivering the solution, e.g., will it be outsourced, developed in-house, or in partnership with others. Is it a completely new solution or an extension of an existing solution? The Project Approach Questionnaire (PAQ) is used to identify any risks associated with using the agile PM approach.

By the end of the Foundations phase, the project manager must ensure that the Management Approach Definition defines the approach for delivering the solution. The PAQ will be revised and all outstanding risks for the approach must be managed.

Foundations Summary

In the Foundations Summary, the results of the Foundations phase are presented to the business sponsor and all high-level stakeholders (often in the form of a presentation). They should be able to decide whether there is sufficient justification to move into the Development phase.

Evolving Solution

The Evolving Solution depends entirely on the goals of the project and the current project phase. Products may be at different stages of development (e.g., "in progress," completed, partial solution, or similar) It may include models, prototypes, supporting materials, and test and safety records. It is created by the Solution Development Team.

Timebox plan

The Timebox Plan is an evolutionary product that takes the not-yet-detailed timebox requirements from the Delivery Plan and provides more detail and depth. It is created by the Solution Development Team and often takes the form of a team board showing work to be done, work in progress, and work completed ("To Do", "Doing", "Done"). It is updated at the Daily Standup.

Timebox Review Record

The Timebox Review Record is an evolutionary product that captures the feedback of each review in a timebox and describes the progress to that review. This is a governance product and can be as formal or informal as required. When a structured timebox is used, there is a review for investigation, a review for refinement, and a review for consolidation. It is produced by the team leader.

Project Review Report

At the end of the final deployment, a final retrospective is held and recorded in the Project Review Report. The project is officially closed and it is evaluated from a business, technical and process perspective. The use of Agile Project Management is reviewed and processes are optimized for future projects.

Benefits Assessment

In many cases, no further planning is done for the post-project phase and no further evaluation takes place at the end of the project. If the product is deployed in multiple steps, it is possible to start the Benefits Assessment before the final deployment and then feed any suggestions for changes or improvements back into the ongoing project.

The Benefits Assessment describes how the benefits have actually accrued when the deployed solution is operational. The main objective is to assess whether benefits have been realized. If the business case indicated that the benefits are expected to accrue over a longer period of time, there may be several reviews.

This also gives the organization the opportunity to address any discrepancies between expected and actual results. Where a program or portfolio management is the client of a project, the Benefits Assessment often falls within their scope of activities and is managed by them.

TEN

AGILE CONTROL

One advantage of an agile approach is that a project manager is warned of problems early on, possibly after the first two weeks of development. It becomes apparent that remedial action needs to be taken, and optimism that problems are temporary and things will get better is avoided early on. When a project is behind schedule early on, it usually ends up being at least that far behind, usually more. Yet teams and project managers continue to believe that things will improve.

Sometimes early warnings can even indicate that a project is failing at the beginning. This provides an opportunity to stop failing projects before more time and money are lost.

The project manager and team leader must constantly review and respond to any issues that may affect the project.

When a problem occurs, it is important that the completion date remains unchanged, as the whole approach is about on-time delivery. Once this has passed, it cannot be fixed in the future. From the beginning, teams and project managers need to protect the agreed delivery deadline and look for other ways to solve the problem.

The first choice will always be to delete the least important feature from the timebox or from the project, or both. Sometimes, given the current situation, it is necessary to revise the list of prioritized requirements.

It is important for stakeholders to understand that while Agile accepts change, it changes the depth of requirements that do not change the breadth. Adding new "must have" requirements is seen as changing the breadth and scope of the project.

This is not what the early estimates were based on, and for this reason, new "must haves" require formal change control.

Risk Management

Risk management in Agile is no different from other project management approaches. A risk log is required and should be reviewed regularly.

Risks must be identified, assessed for severity, impact and priority, and then countermeasures proposed, planned and regularly reviewed. This is normal risk management.

Agile project management reduces some classic waterfall risks: Using the MoSCoW technique to prioritize requirements and the ability to accommodate change ensures that the right solution is created. Testing is done as early as possible and continuously through iterative development.

However, agile project management comes with some different risks than traditional project management, which are associated with the principles and the instrumental success factors. These must be closely monitored and the entire team is responsible for ensuring that the principles are adhered to. A key principle is to ensure that there is strong collaboration between roles with a business focus and those with a technical focus. If this is not the case, the likelihood that the solution development team will be able to appropriately deliver the solutions needed "by the business" is reduced.

If there is a very detailed design up front and 100% of the solution is expected, the benefits of using MoSCoW technology are limited and time and cost cannot be balanced.

Using small, highly collaborative teams means that a lot of verbal communication may be required and changes to the team may result in the new member not understanding the background of the decisions made.

The entire team should be aware of the risks, but it is the project manager who drives risk management.

The Project Approach Questionnaire (PAQ) helps identify potential risk areas. After completion in Foundations, a check should be made for each Development Timebox to see if the risk profile for the project has changed.

Requirements Management

A requirement is a service, benefit, or function that the user wants the solution to have or perform.

Requirements are often described in the form of a "user story". User stories are short, simple descriptions of a feature told from the perspective of the person who wants the new feature, usually a user or customer of the product. They usually follow a simple template:

*As a [**role**], I need [**the requirement or function**] so that [**benefits can be achieved**].*

Such requirements are often written in very general terms and are only further refined and broken down into sub-requirements in the course of development. Thus, a user story can be divided into one, two or even dozens of user stories, which have different priorities and scopes and are realized at different points in time in the project or, if necessary, are omitted entirely based on their priority.

The structure of a user story is chosen because it not only makes clear who the beneficiary of a requirement is and what it is, but also provides a guide for prioritization through the benefits presented.

The requirements evolve and become more detailed in each lifecycle phase. By the end of the Feasibility phase, there are usually fewer than ten requirements, by the end of the Foundations phase there are up to one hundred, and by the end of the Evolutionary Development phase there are often well over one hundred.

A large number of requirements defined too early is seen as a risk for agile project management, as this indicates too much detail too early. This is referred to as a "Big Design Up Front", which would be more sought after in a traditional project management approach.

The list of prioritized requirements is agreed upon by the business sponsor and relevant stakeholders.

Ideally, an initial small number of coarse requirements, from the Feasibility phase, will be expanded to the next level of detail during the Foundations phase. The low level detail is expanded and clarified just prior to execution of the work.

If low-level details are not formalized too early, flexibility is possible throughout the scope without the need for formal change control.

The requirements must cover the requirements of the product as well as the functional requirements and the non-functional requirements.

Functional requirements describe what is required, not how it should be delivered. For example, a functional requirement would be that a system must clarify that both a correct billing address and a correct shipping address exist for every online order. However, it should not be determined how this verification will be performed, for example, whether an external address database will be included or verification algorithms will be implemented, etc. This will be verified by the Solution Development Team. If solutions are specified too early, this may limit innovation.

A related non-functional requirement may be that the address check may take a maximum of 2 seconds.

User Stories

A user story is one of the most common ways to express a requirement. It is always written from the end user's point of view.

Requirements at a high level of abstraction are sometimes referred to as epics. These are large user stories that can be divided into several smaller stories. An epic is usually too large to fit into a timebox. Epics are usually held in the Feasibility phase. By the end of the Foundations phase, they must be broken down enough to fit more than one User Story into a Timebox.

All user stories have the same format. They should be written from the perspective of the role that will be used or impacted by the solution, and defined in language relevant to that role. This helps clarify the true reason for the requirement. The idea is not to go into low-level details too early, and they should be intentionally short to encourage conversation about the stories.

User Stories - The 3-C Approach

- **Card** - the card - with which the request can be recorded
- **Conversation** - The conversation - which is generated from the user story
- **Confirmation** - these are the acceptance criteria noted on the back of the card as questions that expect a yes answer and contain the non-functional requirements.

The point here is that requirements are not simply accepted and passed on, but that it is of central importance that the content of the user story has first been understood. Different people often have a different use of language. Only when it can be ensured that the content of the requirement has been understood can implementation also be target-oriented. To confirm this, it is clarified with the stakeholder what his central requirements are and what the quality characteristics are from his point of view. It may well be that different stakeholders have different ideas here. It is worth clarifying these before working on the implementation of the story.

User Stories - INVEST Pattern

Another quality requirement for good user stories is described under the acronym INVEST pattern. It was originally developed by Bill Wake as a quality attribute for good requirements in the context of the agile method XP (eXtreme Programming), but is now used by many agile methods. It provides guidance for creating well-constructed user stories.

- **I** - The I stands for Independent because each story should stand on its own and be as independent as possible from other stories.
- **N** - The N stands for Negotiable, where conversation is important. The stories are placeholders that the team will explore in more detail during evolutionary development.
- **V** - The V stands for Valuable. Stories should represent features that have obvious business value to the user.
- **E** - The E stands for Estimable. Any story should be clear enough to estimate the time scales for development. Included in this requirement is that questions must be largely clarified. Only when the questions are clarified to the extent that a development team can imagine a solution path is a meaningful estimate possible.
- **S** - S stands for Small because stories should be small enough to estimate from. If this is not the case, they should be divided into smaller stories.
- **T** - T stands for Testable, which means that they must be formulated clearly and specifically enough to be testable.

A well-written user story does not combine, overlap, or conflict with other stories. It conforms to organizational standards and guidelines where appropriate, is driven by business requirements expressed in business case and project goals, and when multiple stories refer to the same feature, they reference each other.

The Business Analyst

The Business Analyst is responsible for requirements-related documentation, which is particularly important given the evolutionary nature of agile project management for requirements. He or she ensures that only requirements that impact the depth of the project are added after the Foundations phase. Changes in breadth should be handled formally or informally, depending on the nature of the project. It is important to keep track of this to prevent shifting the project focus.

The Business Analyst is responsible for ensuring that requirements are properly analyzed and that the Solution Development team understands how they are driving the development effort. S/he ensures that the right people are involved in the business to effectively communicate with the technical roles of the project. They are not expected to be the "voice" of the business, but rather ensure that the right people are being approached.

The Business Analyst helps the business think through and understand the full implications of the requirements.

There should be close collaboration between the Business Analyst, the Business Ambassador and the Solution Tester.

The business analyst should have the skills to identify dependencies, overlaps, and conflicts between requirements and their impact on business goals and overall organizational alignment.

Estimate

Estimates are used for a variety of purposes to evaluate the business case, assess feasibility, understand project costs, or create overview-level schedules. They are a communication tool with stakeholders.

Agile project management estimation is about asking, "How long do we have?", "What resources do we have?" and then figuring out how to achieve the goal within time and cost constraints. Traditional projects typically try to figure out how long the entire project will take before starting work.

Agile project management makes estimating easier because only fixed estimates are made for the next increment, not for the entire project.

The MoSCoW technique includes the possibility to cover the risk of the unknown. Where early estimates may have been too optimistic because not enough was known at the time, here the estimates are constantly reviewed. The accuracy of the estimates should improve as the project progresses and the understanding of the requirements deepens.

Estimates should always be seen in the context of the current project phase. At the end of the Feasibility phase, the estimates are just sufficient to justify the early business case and the planning required for the Foundations phase.

At the end of the Foundations phase, estimates are based on more in-depth research, but they should not be too precise. It is sufficient if they show whether the business case is still justified and the Delivery Plan needs to be created. This Delivery Plan contains a schedule with timeboxes for the delivery of the project.

During development, each timebox informs more accurate estimates for the next timebox. Agile project management makes estimating easier. It only needs to make fixed estimates for the next increment, not for the entire project.

By delivering timeboxes frequently, actual results can be verified earlier, so estimates can be revised and improved through inspection and adjustment. Typically, at the end of a two-week timebox, there is feedback on how good or bad the estimates were, so that this knowledge can be incorporated into the estimation of the next timebox. It is easier to estimate what can be done within a fixed timebox, say within two weeks, than to estimate how long it will take to complete something in its entirety.

Feasibility and foundation estimates are top-down estimates. At these early stages there are many unknowns and for this reason the estimates cannot be accurate.

At the end of Foundations, the middle requirement stage, more is known, so now you can commit to the deadline via the delivery schedule.

During development, a more accurate bottom-up estimate is made based on a more detailed specification of the work to be implemented.

The Cone of Uncertainty [1] describes how the degree of uncertainty decreases as more research and development is done and more information is obtained about the project.

Uncertainty tends to decrease until the end of the project when all risks have been terminated or transferred.

[1] Wikipedia writes (accessed 5/2020):

The Cone of Uncertainty describes the progression of uncertainties in a project. It goes back to a study by NASA, which found that an estimate made at the beginning of the project life cycle (i.e., before the requirements phase) is still loaded with an uncertainty of a factor of 4 on average. For example, the "actual" time required for a project can be four times as long or even only a quarter as long as originally estimated.

This factor varies depending on the character of the project: the larger the share of research and development, the higher the uncertainty.

The uncertainty decreases steadily over the course of the project, but does not reach 0% until the end of the project. The name "Cone of Uncertainty" is derived from the fact that the uncertainty curve initially drops sharply and then gradually approaches 0.

Consequences of the Cone of Uncertainty:

- An estimate of time, cost and quality at the beginning of the project can at best provide a rough guide
- Estimates for the creation of a project plan and thus the project plan itself should be updated regularly
- Uncertainties can be directly included in the estimates (see two-time method, three-time method)
- If possible, the project plan should include and reflect the uncertainties

ELEVEN

SUCCESS FACTORS AND ADAPTATION POSSIBILITIES OF DSDM

The Project Approach Questionnaire (PAQ) - Assessing Options and Risks

Since DSDM can be used for very different types and sizes of projects, it is important to get an overview of the project, the requirements and the framework conditions and then adapt the approach accordingly. This approach is a prerequisite for a project management methodology to be versatile and is virtually standard. In order to get an overview of the most important aspects and thus have a basis for adaptation, DSDM has developed a questionnaire, called PAQ or Project Approach Questionnaire. A download version of the English edition can be found as an Excel sheet for free download on the website:

https://www.agilebusiness.org/page/ProjectFramework_19_AppendixBProjectApproachQuestionnaire

Working with the PAQ should not be a one-time procedure, but should be repeated in the later project phases after an initial recording in the feasibility phase, since some risks only arise in a certain project phase or have already been eliminated or reduced in a certain phase. Some organizations have adapted the PAQ to include other aspects and risks relevant to their projects.

The following are the statements of the PAQ and their relevance to the adaptations of the DSDM approach.

Statement 1: "All members of the project understand and accept the DSDM approach (philosophy, principles and practices)."

Many users of a methodology first try a cherry-picking approach. Things are sorted out, some are added or rewritten. When we talk about adapting the DSDM approach, this is not what we mean. Adjustments to circumstances are useful in any management, but they should always be based on an "informed basis." Only when interrelationships are understood can adjustments to elements be estimated. Accordingly, it is important to carry out projects with people who are trained in the DSDM method and can understand and estimate interrelationships. Knowledge can also be imparted and supported by involving experts.

Statement 2: "The Business Sponsor and Business Visionary clearly and proactively take ownership of the project."

In any project, leadership support is essential. This allows obstacles to be removed more easily, decisions to be reached in a timely manner, and needed resources and funding to be obtained. If it cannot be ensured that the roles defined by leadership also have sufficient awareness and support for the project, the project should be put on hold until appropriate support is in place. This is the only way to ensure that the products produced will also be in accordance with the client and will meet the intended benefits.

Statement 3: "The corporate vision behind the project is clearly stated and understood by all members of the project team."

It is of central importance for the success of a project that decisions can be made at all levels. This presupposes that there is a common understanding of the goal. If this is not the case, decisions are not made in line with the corporate vision or it becomes necessary for some roles, for example the project manager, to wear themselves out in micromanagement and thus not have the time available for the higher-level work and decisions.

If it is determined that this issue exists, the Business Visionary should be asked to ensure that such a shared corporate vision exists and that it is communicated and shared with stakeholders.

Statement 4: "All project participants understand and accept the importance of submitting an acceptable solution on time as a primary success factor."

On-time delivery is an important quality feature of a product. Delayed delivery and commissioning can lead to a considerable reduction in benefits. In projects where there are no external requirements for a specific delivery date, such a date should nevertheless be defined within the project in order not to lose focus and get lost in trivialities without a significant contribution to the benefit. Apart from that, the definition of a specific delivery time is also linked to the business case. Later delivery in most cases means higher costs (personnel, resources, financial costs), which influences the business case and thus the planned benefit.

Statement 5: "Requirements can be prioritized and there is confidence in meeting agreed costs and deadlines by varying the scope of the solution presented."

The MoSCoW rule should be followed for prioritizing requirements. There should be a possibility of flexibility within the details of the requirements. Requirements can be subdivided into sub-requirements, which do not necessarily all have the same prioritization as the original overall requirement. Also a work with contingency time boxes is conceivable in the connection, in which the conversion of requirements of lower priority are intended, which can be used however elsewhere, if it does not succeed to convert sufficiently requirements of higher priority. One could therefore speak of a kind of "buffer". This approach makes it possible, despite possible delays in the implementation of some requirements, to still meet the planned delivery date.

Statement 6: "All members of the project team accept the only rough definition of the requirements during the initial phase and the announcement of the details only during the development"

If all details are to be defined at the start of the project, this has a negative impact on the possibility of implementing findings made during the project, or efforts to determine requirements have to be written off. Defining details too early increases the risk of being inaccurate. Changing requirements (especially at the detail level) can have a wide variety of reasons, for example:

- Changes in legal or regulatory requirements
- Changes in corporate strategy
- Changes in the market or with customers
- Newly acquired knowledge
- Technological changes
- Changes to products or areas with which interfaces exist
- u.v.a.

It is worthwhile to determine together in the discussion what level of detail makes sense at what point in time. It is also important that there is always a willingness to change requirements and especially their details if this leads to better customer benefits.

Statement 7: "All members of the project team accept the inevitability of changes to requirements and that the right solution can only be delivered if changes are welcomed."

The agile manifesto states: "Responding to change more than following a plan". In order to use DSDM meaningfully, it is important to do so in the context of projects where all participants agree that the project is not about working through a fixed list of requirements, but about creating a solution of maximum customer benefit within a time, cost and quality framework. However, this can very often only be identified more precisely in the course of the project. Accordingly, the definition of detailed specifications should be delayed as much as possible in order to be able to use as much knowledge as possible from the incremental approach.

Statement 8: "The Business Sponsor and Business Visionary understand the importance of active business involvement, and they are willing and empowered to commit appropriate business resources to the project."

Unlike traditional approaches, where all requirements are recorded in detail before the project begins, this makes little sense in an agile context. If requirements can change in the course of a project based on findings and changed framework conditions, etc., it does not make sense to stretch considerable effort into requirements elicitation (which may no longer be relevant in the course of the project). Detailed specifications are coordinated between company representatives and the project team during the course of the project. For this purpose, it is particularly necessary that the Business Ambassador and the Business Advisor can provide corresponding capacities.

Statement 9: "It is possible for the Solution Development Team members responsible for business and solution development to collaborate throughout the project."

In a context where requirements evolve, questions arise which often have to be decided quickly in order not to cause a standstill in the project. Often, there is also a need to adapt framework conditions to new circumstances. This requires close cooperation of all persons and roles involved in the development. Ideally, the roles with a business focus are also available for questions and decisions at any time. Joint collaboration is crucial for evolutionary solution development. Maximum customer benefit can only be achieved from combinations of people with different backgrounds of experience. Availability should also be taken into account when planning timeboxes, and where geography makes collaboration difficult, ways must be sought to optimally bridge these obstacles. Electronic aids such as video conferencing, virtual team boards or the like can greatly simplify communication in such cases.

Statement 10: "All Solution Development Team members are appropriately and sufficiently empowered to support the day-to-day decision making necessary for rapid solution

development within the context of short, focused timboxes."

Each member of the Solution Development Team must have the necessary knowledge and experience, but also the appropriate authority to make day-to-day decisions within the scope of their job. Where this is not the case, there is a risk of a bottleneck due to micromanagement. It makes sense to jointly define a framework of authority and make it transparent. Where this is difficult, for example, based on other corporate and decision-making structures, an appropriate procedure can also be agreed and implemented step by step in order to create trust through the hierarchy and self-confidence among the members of the Solution Development Team.

Statement 11: "DSDM roles and responsibilities have been assigned in an appropriate manner and all stakeholders understand and accept the responsibilities associated with their role."

DSDM's role model is built to fit both very large and small projects. To make this possible in everyday life, DSDM offers the possibility that one person can also hold several roles, or that one role (not all, but most) can be held by several people.

When a person assumes a role, he or she must know its responsibilities and be able to carry them out. To this end, it is appropriate to offer appropriate training measures. Roles may only be taken on by people who feel that they are up to the demands placed on them (professionally, personally, in terms of time). Where it is not clear which persons are suitable for certain roles, it is worth involving the DSDM coach as the bearer of the necessary expertise in order to clarify any questions.

Statement 12: "The Solution Development Team has appropriate shared knowledge and skills (soft and technical skills) to work together to develop an optimal business solution."

In addition to the professional competencies of the members of the Solution Development Team, their social competencies are also of great importance. Within the scope of development activities, people with very different professional and personal backgrounds and at different hierarchical levels work together. In order to work successfully here, it is important that the various participants work together in a goal-oriented manner, respecting each other and being prepared to recognize and value the competencies and skills of the other participants. In order to ensure that an optimal solution can be developed, it is worth investing in the development and expansion of the competencies of the team members in the form of training and coaching, both in technical terms and with regard to their social skills.

Statement 13: "Solution Development Team members are assigned to the project at an appropriate and consistent level sufficient to fully support the DSDM process for establishing timeboxes."

In principle, DSDM assumes that the members of the Solution Development Team are available to the project on a full-time basis. If this is not the case, it should be agreed that the project has priority in any case, so that timebox planning can also be reliable and agreed goals are achievable.

When planning timeboxes, the availability of those involved should always be clarified and used for planning. Where availability cannot be clearly agreed, the tasks of the relevant person should not be firmly scheduled, but only stated as a goal. If this is not acceptable to the business sponsor, the use of other resources, for example through contracted suppliers, may have to be considered.

Statement 14: "The tools and common working practices within the Solution Development Team are sufficient to enable effective, iterative development of the solution."

Capabilities and framework conditions must support iterative solution development. Methodological procedures such as facilitated workshops and modeling & prototyping can be used just as sensibly as technical support measures, for example when teams work at different locations.

Statement 15: "All necessary review and testing activities are fully integrated into iterative development."

In principle, we assume in the context of iterative development that all tasks are performed within an iteration which are necessary to produce a finished partial solution. This is not always possible. Where this is not the case, it can make sense for a second team to test the implemented partial solutions in each case in the context of a test that is staggered by a timebox. Nevertheless, as much testing activity as possible should remain with the original development team. To ensure cross-team compatibility of solution and test design, the Technical Coordinator should be involved. In any case, it should always be taken into account that any delay with regard to testing leads to an increase in project risk.

Statement 16: "Project progress is measured primarily by incremental, demonstrable delivery of business value."

It is not the completion of developer hours that brings a benefit to the customer, but exclusively the implementation of requirements. Accordingly, the progress of a project is not linked to the number of hours (or other resources) used, but to the extent to which the business benefit for the customer has been increased.

During the presentation of the solution increment at the end of the timebox, stakeholders can be kept up to date on the progress of the development and see for themselves how benefits have been realized. Presenting the solution increment is a central activity in the project. Not only does it build trust on the part of the customer, but it also provides an opportunity to learn and develop better, more beneficial solutions based on the resulting conversations. Participants in the presentation should be anyone whose feedback will be useful in optimizing the solution. In addition, this can also strengthen stakeholder buy-in.

Statement 17: "There are no mandatory standards or other constraints that prevent the application of DSDM philosophy and practices to this project."

In the normal course of business, many rules and regulations exist. Some may contradict DSDM's approach. For example, in some places there are standard contracts that require fixed prices for fixed specifications, or there may be internal standards or regulations that could restrict the use or full benefit of DSDM. It makes sense to clarify the current situation and define clear agreements and framework conditions before starting a project with DSDM. To this end, it may be useful to contact the relevant bodies in advance or, if necessary, to involve them in the project as business advisors.

Afterword

We have now looked at the elements of AgilePM, the roles and responsibilities, the processes, the tools, the products and values. We have seen where DSDM sees risks and where success factors are. I hope this has motivated you to look deeper into the subject matter. In the years that I have been using DSDM myself in consulting projects with customers, I have done this with a wide variety of companies and projects. Some were IT projects, some were based in completely different contexts, some involved millions, and others involved projects in the 5-figure euro range. AgilePM offers the possibility to meet all conceivable use cases by adapting to the project circumstances. However, you will not be able to run successful projects by reading books. Whether that is my little book or a DSDM manual. As mostly in life, success lies in experience and practice.

If I have aroused your interest, I cordially invite you to look for a DSDM specialist in your area who will accompany you through the first steps of your project. When choosing, make sure that the person in question has proven theoretical knowledge in the form of certifications, but on the other hand also references from real projects. Only someone who knows both parts will really be able to help you. There are several certifications on the subject of DSDM, which are awarded by the international certifier APMG on behalf of DSDM[1].

Personally, I am deeply convinced of DSDM and highly recommend you to take a look at this exciting methodology if you are looking for a pragmatic project management approach that combines all the advantages of agile product development with those of classic project control. Give the method a chance: you will not regret it.

The author

[1] There are currently certifications for AgilePM (Project Manager), AgileBA (Business Analyst) and for the topic AgileDS (Digital Services) at Foundation and Practitioner level, as well as an AgilePgM (Program Management) Foundation certification in the APMG portfolio. I have taken all of these in the past few years and was able to learn a lot in preparation. The investment in time certainly makes sense in terms of executing your first DSDM project.

CPSIA information can be obtained
at www.ICGtesting.com
Printed in the USA
LVHW020103290423
745602LV00005B/885

9 798888 158128